Looking at Cities

By Margaret Clyne and Rachel Griffiths

This is a city.

Cities have tall buildings.

3

Cities have busy streets.

Cities have many shops.

Cities have big parks.

Cities have people everywhere.

London, England

Sydney, Australia

New York City, United States

Ottawa, Canada

Singapore, Singapore

Buenos Aires, Argentina

There are cities all over the world.